Beautifying Sins

Kiawana Leaf

Foreword By: Pastor Joseph Brown

Beautifying Sins
WRITTEN BY: Kiawana Leaf
© 2020
ALL RIGHTS RESERVED. No part of this book may be reproduced in any written, electronic, recording, or photocopying without written permission of the publisher or author. The exception would be in the case of brief quotations embodied in the critical articles or reviews and pages where permission is specifically granted by the publisher or author.
PUBLISHED BY: Pen Legacy, LLC
TYPESETTING & LAYOUT BY: Junnita Jackson
COVER BY: Christian Cuan
STORY EDITING BY: Carla Dean
Library of Congress Cataloging – in- Publication Data has been applied for.
ISBN: 978-1-7348278-9-7
PRINTED IN THE UNITED STATES OF AMERICA.

Table of Contents

Foreword	1
Introduction	5
What Is Sin?	8
Beautified Sin	16
Acknowledge Your Weakness	19
Embracing Weakness	23
HELP!	27
Why Me?	28
About Me	32
I'm Bruised	36
Honor Thy Father and Mother	41
CONFUSED	46
Shattered	49
Processing	52
Lost	57
Not Ordinary	61
Cleansing	62
Repentance	67
Beautifully Free	72
Acknowledgements	101
About The Author	103

Foreword

Beseeching the Lord concerning growth, change and wholeness requires the unadulterated truth. People in general avoid pain and conflict, but introspection and transparency are imperative when one is striving for contentment and a state of unbrokenness.

In Christ Jesus, we not only find a refuge, but we find someone who will never reject us. Many have been busy searching in the wrong places utilizing the wrong tools to try and fill a place within that can only be filled by our Lord. I have come to learn that the space in us is made complete when we allow the Lord to be our refuge. In the Hebrew language, the word "refuge" is translated from the word "machasech" which means "stronghold; shelter; protection".

During Jesus Christ's time on the earth, he taught others, performed miracles and ensured that the gospel was spread. The last week of His life, He performed the greatest miracle and sacrifice of all, when He suffered for our sins and laid down His life. Matthew 27:50 exclaimed that "He gave up the ghost". He chose to release His life that we may find life! He took upon Himself the sins of the world and suffered for each one of us. In the garden of Gethsemane, Jesus felt the weight of every sin and pain of every person who has ever lived. He was betrayed, arrested, and crucified on the cross. This was a sacrifice only He could make, and He did it willingly so that we can experience Him as our refuge.

When we allow Him to be our refuge, we first experience Him as a stronghold. A stronghold is simply a fortified place. After accepting Him as Lord of our lives, the aim is to make Him a stronghold in our life. Nahum 1:7 in the New American Standard Bible declares "The Lord is good; a stronghold in the day of trouble, And He knows those who take refuge in Him". When we experience God's forgiveness, we begin a process of making Him our refuge or a fortified place. A fortified place may sound restrictive, but it is actually liberating just like the forgiveness of God! Knowing that a slate has been wiped clean and being able to enjoy the beauty of holiness with the Father is inwardly satisfying. Being free from past sins and transgressions is simply a gift. To no longer be tormented by yesterday that I may enjoy today and look forward to tomorrow is a present that should never be taken for granted.

When we allow the Lord to be our refuge, we then experience Him as our shelter. Experiencing the joy of salvation and knowing that no matter who we were or what vice was our friend, the love of Christ welcomed us and provided a shelter that will never be removed. The irrevocable love of Christ is steadfast, sure and strong. This is the kind of love that teaches you that you are greater than what you did and that your future is filled with endless possibilities. He loves you back to the person He always knew you could be. When the love of Christ washes over you, your vision change and you have a new view of yourself and of others. You love yourself differently; you distribute grace and forgiveness easier and you love life in a new and unimaginable way.

When we allow the Lord to be our refuge, we then experience Him as our protection. Part of God's stamp of beautifying our sins is to provide protection from a myriad of things including ourselves. On our journey to wholeness, He will address the root of what lead us to a place of sin or a negative habitual lifestyle. I have come to learn that there are times when people stay in cycles of sin and ungodly places it is because there are some unaddressed areas that have not been touched by God. Allowing Him to be your protection gives you a refuge from yourself. Paul said in Galatians 2:20, I am crucified with Christ: nevertheless I live; yet not I, but Christ liveth in me: and the life which I now live in the flesh I live by the faith of the Son of God, who loved me, and gave himself for me. As Christ crucifies our flesh so that it humbles us, He then beautifies the meek with salvation and become a permanent refuge for us in the time of trouble or the season of temptation.

Beautifying sins documents for us a transparent, thrilling and triumphant young ingenue who has done the work and continues to do the work of a life that screams Psalm 91:2 - I will say of the LORD, He is my refuge and my fortress: my God; in him will I trust. Truly, she is an example of how the Lord takes the guilty and make them innocent again. Kiawana shows us through her second work, "Beautifying Sins" that her journey has not always been a bed of roses, but if you allow God to be your refuge, He can take the barren, broken and bruised places of life and birth amazing fruit to inspire growth and change all around you.

Pastor Joseph L. Brown
House of Healing DMV –Inc.

Introduction

"Christ suffered for our sins once for all time. He never sinned, but He died for sinners to bring you safely home to God. He suffered physical death, but He was raised to life in the Spirit."
1 Peter 3:18

If you are anything like me, you are questioning the title. How do you beautify a sin? It sounds crazy and impossible, right? What if it is possible to beautify a sin? As I am writing this, I, too, am quite puzzled by the idea of beautifying sins! I am stretched and challenged throughout this journey. I'm also curious. How exactly does one beautify a sin?

Even though I am living my life in sin, could there possibly be beauty in this? What would make my sin beautiful? I'm sure a thousand questions are flowing through your mind. How can the impossible be possible?

Will you allow me to be transparent, authentic, and non-judgmental with you? Can you adjust your lenses and understand the purpose of sins to see how we are able to make our ugly truths a beautiful thing? Do you accept my challenge to beautify your sins?

You may be reading this book as a result of being intrigued by the title. It is possible you are curious about how you can beautify a sin. Or you're one who admits that you are guilty of your sins and wants to be made anew, seeking the answer to how you can make your ugly past a beautiful thing. Or maybe you're the non-believer who lives their life by no book or rules, believing there is absolutely nothing wrong with you. Does your life fall into the "I'm just here for the comments" social media category?

If Confidence Unlocked inspired you, I'm sure you will be able to relate to the content of this book even more. I challenge my returning readers to dig a little bit deeper into beautifying sins! Dig a lot deeper. Completely remove your mask and be free. That is what I am doing. So, I ask you again, "Do you accept my challenge to beautify your sins?"

Throughout your journey and this challenge, know that I am always here with you. You may be just beginning or going through, but rest assured you are not alone! I am not perfect. I make mistakes, and I am pressing further through the challenge along with you.

I don't know your story, and you're just getting to know mine. There's no space in healing or freedom for judgement. I promise you that we will all evolve and win together! I have faith and vision in the impossible. However, before you dig into Beautifying Sins and get started with this challenge, let's first identify what sin is exact

What Is Sin?

Merriam-Webster's Dictionary defines sin as "an offense against religious or moral law; an action that is or is felt to be highly reprehensible; an often serious shortcoming: FAULT. It then goes on to say, "transgression of the law of God; a vitiated state of human nature in which the self is estranged from God." What beauty could possibly result from committing a sin, offense, or being at fault?

What is your definition of sin?
_____
_____
_____
_____
_____

If you are a believer, I imagine one of the first things that come to mind when characterizing sin is the Ten Commandments. Unfortunately, we live in a society where the concept of sin is expressed in legalistic arguments rather than right and wrong. When we consider sin, we immediately think of disobeying Biblical law, the Ten Commandments. We emphasize murder and adultery while dismissing lying, cursing, and idolatry, not realizing that is not all to defining sin.

Can you be honest with yourself and admit that you are a sinner? It would be interesting to know how many people thought to themselves, or either said aloud, "I'm not a sinner!" If we were to face our truths, we would all acknowledge that we are sinners. Whether you want to admit it or not, you, me, and everyone we know are sinners! Sin is not just violating the Ten Commandments. Sin is the failure to live our lives in perfection, just as Christ did. No one is perfect in all their ways except for God, so how could you possibly not be a sinner?

Psalms 18:30 tells us, "God's way is perfect," and again in 2 Samuel 22:31, we are reminded, "God's way is perfect," along with many more passages in the Bible.

It doesn't say Kiawana, Julian, Tiffany, Bryan, and so forth are perfect. Realistically, we are all sinners. Perfect is impossible for any man to reach. We sing aloud, "God, you're perfect in all of your ways!" To dig a little deeper, Webster's Dictionary told us sin is a fault. How often do we take responsibility for an accident or misfortune? When do we accept accountability for the unattractive, unsatisfactory, and toxic ways in our character? Do we admit that we've been misguided, leaving the effect of dangerous actions or habits? How often are we critical of others for their inadequacy or mistakes? Are we guilty of finding fault in others rather than examining ourselves in the mirror?

If perfection is impossible, how can our sins become beautiful? How are we capable of beautifying sins? I'm sure you are probably wondering, and I'm glad you are.

Let's go back a little. I asked for you to write your definition of sin. Why are we trained to believe that sin only involves the Ten Commandments?

> *I am the Lord your God*
> - *You will not have no other God before Me*
> - *You will not make no image of God*
> - *You will not use the Lord's name in vain*
> - *Remember to keep the Sabbath day Holy*
> - *Honor thy father and mother*
> - *You will not kill*
> - *You will not commit adultery*
> - *You will not steal*
> - *You will not testify falsely against your neighbor*
> - *You will not covet your neighbor's goods*

Those who have not murdered or committed adultery will surely find themselves at fault for lying or worshipping false idols, like wealth or power, ahead of God. I know I have found myself convicted in my spirit of lying repeatedly and acting as though money or wealth was all I needed. I was at fault in many situations, but I did not accept responsibility. I was working a nine-to-five doing cosmetology and even hustling drugs in the streets. Wealth was the most important thing to me. I, honestly, was not thinking about putting God first. I wanted the latest labels. I wanted to live a life that I wanted to live. I did the things I wanted to do.

It does us no good to compare ourselves to others. Your story may be similar to mine, but you cannot compare yourself to me. We can't escape our wrongdoings by looking at them next to the wrongdoings of others. It's crazy how God works. It's only when we understand our weaknesses that we can rely on the sacrifice of Jesus and cry out to God, saying, "Father God, give me strength!" The strength and power that He gives us in our weaknesses are all satisfactory for His glory.

Sin gets a little deeper because we battle with temptation. On the one hand, we strive to be like Christ or live a better life by making better decisions. On the other hand, we are fighting our human flesh. Keep it real with yourself. I know this journey is a battle for me. Your struggle may not look like mine, but I am almost certain you have a battle, whether it is with money, sex, power, or something else. The greatest tempter, the enemy, will use deceit to convince us that our flesh-driven desires are not in conflict with God's desires for us. As a result of this deception, any of us will begin to believe it is acceptable to become comfortable with our sin without admitting that we are sinners.

Society makes it harder for us to face our truths and remove our masks. We are encouraged to display, even celebrate, sin. Pay attention to the lyrics of today's popular music, the scripts of movies, the depictions of award-winning television shows, and even some of the doctrine preached in the churches. We love to see how close we can get without actively sinning. Once tempted, we are easily influenced to sin.

Can you face temptation and remain without sin? Why or why not?

_____
_____
_____
_____
_____

Now let's get a little personal:
Why do you sin?

_____
_____
_____
_____
_____

The result of our minds agreeing with lust or desiring in our flesh is sin! Sin is a choice; it is something we choose to do. Sin is what we agree upon in a lustful or pleasurable moment – that thing we do in the moment.

I sat back and thought this chapter was complete, but my spirit said, "No, Kiawana, that's not the end. There's still more work for you to do personally, and there is still so much more that needs to be said." As bad as I wanted to describe sin briefly without going too deep, I just couldn't let it go. Just as I asked you to accept the challenge, I had to accept this challenge, also.

I'm pretty sure, despite what I have said, many may still believe they are not sinners or have never sinned. I have been sent to inspire you to face your truths and remove your mask. It is imperative that we understand the word of God so we can all make it into the Kingdom! With that said, I started fasting and praying. I asked God, "What else do you want me to say or do? What am I to add to this chapter that I haven't already said?" Instantly, the spirit responded, "Well, Kiawana, you did not fully answer nor identify your own question in your chapter, What Is Sin? Furthermore, you have to put in the work to beautify your own sins. There is so much more that you did not cover."

I was puzzled. What didn't I cover? What did I need to do? What sin haven't I beautified? How did I not identify all of sin? I realized I had much more work to do, including facing my truths. I had to get more personal and transparent with myself if I were going to be open and authentic with you.

As believers, we generally view sin as an "evil human act that violates the rational nature of man". Sin focuses on how we treat humanity, both ourselves and others, as well as how we respond to God's nature and His eternal law. I know my non-believers are like, "Okay, well, I'm not a believer. So now what, sis?" (Chuckling) No worries! Hold on!

Sin goes deeper than what we know, think, or was taught. I didn't know this, but there is a HUGE umbrella of sin. Did you know there are many different types?

- Actual sin – one of the hardest to avoid; an evil act, whether it's a thought, word, or deed.
- Mortal sin – deliberate turning away from God; a sin that you're knowledgeable of and consent to doing. Until one repents, this cuts you off from God and His grace. Examples of mortal sin are murder, rape, and perjury.
- Formal sin – one that's committed by a person who knows the action is wrong and which causes personal guilt.
- Material sin – an act committed by a person who does not know it to be wrong, and the person is not personally culpable.
- Venial sin – a "lesser" sin that does not result in complete separation from God, as mortal sin does. Venial sin is committed with less self-awareness of wrongdoing. Although this type of sin weakens a union with God, it doesn't completely stop God's grace.

Having gone into the depth of defining sin and its varieties, surely each of us felt convicted by one form of sin, if not more. Whether a believer or non-believer, and whether we want to be real with ourselves or not, none of us are perfect. At least one form of sin has defined all of us in our own guilty way, and that's okay. Acknowledge the wrongdoing, take accountability, embrace it, and begin to make the ugly truths a beautiful thing through change.

"Remember, when you are being tempted, do not say, 'God is tempting me.' God is never tempted to do wrong, and he never tempts anyone else. 14Temptation comes from our own desires, which entice us and drag us away. 15These desires give birth to sinful actions. And when sin is allowed to grow, it gives birth to death." James 1:13-15

With a better understanding of sin, how can we beautify our sins?

Beautified Sin

This can't be a challenge where you just sit back and enjoy your reading. This chapter is where you become the author, remove your mask, and be completely transparent with yourself. Now that we have defined sin, I challenge you to share with yourself and God the unhealthy ways you beautify yourself in sin. How do you beautify your pride, greed, lust, envy, or even gluttony? How do you beautify your toxicity and failure to take accountability? Be open and honest with yourself. Kill the façade. This challenge will not benefit anyone else. Its purpose is to help you in your journey to be free! Dig deep! God would love to hear from you.

Acknowledge Your Weakness

"That's why I take pleasure in my weaknesses, and in the insults, hardships, persecutions, and troubles that I suffer for Christ. For when I am weak, then I am strong." 2 Corinthians 12:10

Am I the only one who dislikes being asked in an interview, "What are some of your weaknesses?" What will we gain from not only acknowledging our weakness but also disclosing them to others? Weakness, just as sin, has various meanings. It is important that we truly understand the definition of weakness. Let's be clear; weakness does not mean we are not good at something. It would be easy to acknowledge that basketball, tennis, or hockey isn't one of our strongest hobbies.

Some of my weaknesses included being self-critical, lacking confidence, and limiting communication until I'm comfortable or trust another. I was also nervous when asking certain questions. Some of my other abysmal characteristics are procrastination, impatience, timidity, and not responding well to criticism.

When frustrated, intimidated, overwhelmed, upset, sad, alone, or depressed, I turned to marijuana and alcohol to help me cope with my nerves and anxiety. Some people need a cigarette when their nerves get bad. That was not me; I was never the cigarette-smoker type of chick. I recall using sexual attraction and sexual pleasure as a coping mechanism when I felt empty in my relationships. Whenever I felt lonely and annoyed in my singleness, I would entertain people with no pure intentions. They were just something to do to distract me. When I felt a void from my father, I would act out, settle, seek attention, or gravitate toward a man to feel that love I desired. I failed to realize I was experiencing pain more than love. I settled for the potential of it turning into love. During arguments or disagreements, the heat would be too hot for me to face my truths. I'd rather lie, make excuses, or blame others than tell the truth and be accountable for my actions. I ran away from what was right for me towards what felt good in the heat of the moment. I was comfortable, complacent, and self-centered. My guilt and shame overpowered me.

My flesh was weak; I lacked self-control and wisdom. I lived my life ungodly and rejected the possibility that I deserved anything good. I was toxic, broken, bitter, and weak in my prayer time. I rarely prayed. I didn't know what to say or even how to pray. My faith was weak. I didn't believe in what I couldn't see. I always tried to be strong even when I was weak and broken on the inside. I was scared, fearful, and prideful, too. There was no way I was going to be meek. That was the weakest of my mentality. I was worried about what he would do or what she would say. I was a people pleaser. Yes, that was me!

Whether you want to admit it or not, you, too, have weaknesses. I've learned that being honest with myself has helped me and many of those around me. I have been transparent and honest with you. I challenge you to face your truths, acknowledge your weaknesses, and list them here.

_____
_____
_____
_____
_____

Determining how to define weakness, of course, depends on how it is used. One definition of weakness would be to lack. Would you agree? We are not always in control. We don't know everything. We need help, and it is perfectly fine to admit it when we do. We all have weaknesses in some areas of our lives, and guess what? That is okay!

I would strongly suggest acknowledging and embracing your weaknesses. Hopefully, you acknowledge your weaknesses by listing them above. If so, the next step is to take time for yourself and reflect on them throughout your journey. How else does one heal, grow, glow, evolve, and become a stronger and better person? Use what hinders you as your greatest weapon!

"Obviously, the law applies to those to whom it was given, for its purpose is to keep people from having excuses, and to show that the entire world is guilty before God. 20For no one can never be made right with God by doing what the law commands. The law simply shows us how sinful we are." Romans 3:19-20 NLT

Embracing Weakness

"Pride goes before destruction, and haughtiness before a fall. 19Better to live humbly with the poor than to share plunder with the proud. 20Those who listen to instruction will prosper; those who trust the Lord will be joyful." Proverbs 16:18-20

Now that we have acknowledged our weaknesses, we can go further. If you are similar to me, pride, self-esteem, fears, and the feeling of not being good enough has a stronghold on you. Is that you, too? What I have discovered in my journey is embracing my weaknesses was the only way I was able to work on them. I had to remove my mask and keep it real with myself if no one else. Embracing my weaknesses has allowed a positive change in my life and created multiple opportunities for my growth.

I encourage you to embrace yours, too. You may be thinking, She keeps saying keep it real with myself! That's absolutely right. Nobody holds us back from being successful but ourselves. I am holding myself accountable to make sure we all win together. I can only share with you what I have personally experienced. Change your weakness to your strengths; unlock your confidence and potential in every aspect of your life.

Do you struggle with low self-esteem, or have you struggled with it in the past? Are you so complacent in toxicity that what should be a positive attribute now causes negativity? The lack of assurance in your judgment, ability, and power has affected your character and self-respect.

I know he/she is no good for me. They hurt me more than complete me, but I don't want to be alone. He/she looks too good to leave. I don't want to see them with anyone else. I don't want to start over. I will miss the materialistic gifts. The sexual pleasures are too good for me. I don't want to feel that void of not having them in my life. I don't want to have to wonder how I will make ends meet. These are common explanations when we are masking our power, excusing our feelings, and justifying our bad judgement. This rationale limits our capability and impedes true happiness and success. Can you agree? Can you relate to this scenario?

Embracing my lack of self-confidence helped me unmask my hidden potential. I removed self-imposed limitations and stopped making excuses for my toxic behavior, creating powerful momentum in my life. I've decided to trust and believe in myself. Now I can achieve anything that I put my heart and mind into. Can I tell you something? Imperfections are a part of being human.

We cloak fears as weaknesses. I remember when I was in a dark place of my life during a toxic relationship. I recall being timid, unable to express myself. I shielded my feelings because it seemed as though showing them only harmed me. I usually end up battling physical, mental, emotional, or verbal abuse after expressing my feelings.

I viewed everything through the lens of the hurt of my abusive relationships. "I'm shy" or "I don't say much" were excuses I used to barricade my feelings. To keep it real with you, I still struggle with this a little to this day. I'm not perfect. I'm on this challenge with you. Am I bad at communicating or just scared to express myself? Is it fear or genuinely a character flaw?

Maybe that scenario isn't your story, but it is an example of how we honestly tend to camouflage a weakness as fear. Embrace your weakness, be honest with yourself, and allow your weakness to guide you to freedom. I have started this journey. It has been one of the hardest things for me to do, but it has been the most rewarding for me.

If you are familiar with Empower Too Inspire®, you're aware that my mission is to inspire many to evolve into their truth, purpose, and power while embracing vulnerability to heal and love themselves unapologetically. Often, we are afraid of appearing weak, or we are scared of showing vulnerability. So, we wear this mask of strength, or we run to refrain from exposing our weakness.

When someone talks to you about your truth, you may respond with denial or become defensive. In my walk to healing, if a toxic trait that became a part of my character were pointed out, I would instantly feel attacked. My feelings would be hurt. Then I would run away from them. I repeated these steps as needed, even while knowing deep down what the person said about me was my truth. I wasn't ready to accept that kind of accountability and face my reality. So, I remained in a cycle of denial and retreat.

I challenge you. Are you ready? We have acknowledged our weaknesses, but are you prepared to embrace them? Will you allow your weakness to guide you to your freedom? A quote that I discovered on social media to be true is, "Embrace your flaws, reduce your ego, and diminish your fears!" -Author unkown

What will you do to embrace your flaws, reduce your ego, and diminish your fear?

_____
_____
_____
_____
_____

We defined sin, acknowledged our weakness, and accepted the challenge to embrace our weakness. How does this help? How can we beautify our sins?

HELP!

I am the lost child who strayed away
The one amongst ninety-nine others that decided to stay
With no desire or thought I'd return some day

I am the lost coin
The one that rolled away
I felt so foreign feeling the feeling of being betrayed

I am the lost daughter and I am in need
But I have sinned against heaven and my Father
The only one who could supply every one of my needs
Now, just how silly of me
I'm no longer worthy to be called daughter
Just hire me as your servant
I don't know what else to do; I just know that I need
HELP!

Why Me?

"God blesses those who patiently endure testing and temptation. Afterward they will receive the crown of life that God has promised to those who love Him." James 1:12

Although I am one who seldom struggled with disobeying the Ten Commandments, I am the one who still battled in formal sin.

Why is God testing me? Why does He allow me to go through trials and tribulations'? Why do I feel like God is setting me up to fail? Why do I feel so empty and numb? Why am I feeling like I'm stuck? I have been doing everything right. Fasting, praying, and even adjusting to walk faithfully in Him. If I am "saved", why am I going through so much? Shouldn't life be easier? Does God not care about me? Why does it seem like non-believers never face anything? I feel as if God wants me to sin purposely!

These were the crazy questions, thoughts, and ideas that were always going through my head. Could you be honest and confess that you have some of these thoughts, too? Have you ever felt like this before?

Unfortunately, during life, we all face obstacles. Whether they manifest in the form of financial problems, physical ailments, childhood trauma, mental issues, grief, distress, fear, loneliness, depression, betrayal, anger, or some other form, obstacles are a part of life. I never understood why, though. Why would God place us in these unfamiliar and uncomfortable situations without us knowing what to do or how to make it through? I can only imagine how amused and upset God gets with us because of our actions in the midst of our tests. Have you ever sat back and thought why not you? What type of glory could come out of this?

On my journey, I learned that how I responded made a big difference during my tests, trials, and tribulations. I thought I was doing everything right, but I wasn't. To cope, I used alcohol, drugs, and addictions. I masked my pain with pride, ego, doubt, and fear, but what good was that? That was nothing but negativity on top of negativity. The whole time I was expecting positivity. How in the world is that possible? Instead of facing my situations, I ran from them and bottled them up inside. I really believed everything would just go away. That's crazy, right?

Nothing good came from my being complacent and afraid of growth. Remaining in my comfort zone kept me in bondage, guilt, shame, and defeat. I was not able to pass my test without learning from it, growing from it, trusting in God, and doing things anew.

After learning a few things about myself, I still didn't understand why God would want to use a little sinner like me. Of all the people in the world, I felt I was least deserving. Why did He still choose little ole Key?

You know the saying, "God calls the unqualified and qualifies the call." Well, that's why you are the chosen one! God shines through His flawed children. God doesn't call perfect people, because perfect people don't exist. He uses ordinary, everyday individuals who battle many conflicts. He uses people who wouldn't have been chosen by this world to be His vessel and magnify His glory and power in this lost and dying world. Why you? So God's glory can shine through you as a trophy of His grace to introduce Him to others or to increase their knowledge of Him.

When you encounter a test, trial, or tribulation, what are some of your first reactions to your situation?

_____
_____
_____
_____
_____

I sense that you're slowly grasping how exactly you can beautify your sins!

"Just look at your own calling, believers; not many (of you were considered) wise according to human standards, not many powerful or influential, not many of high and noble birth. But God has selected (for His purpose) the foolish things of the world to shame the wise (revealing their ignorance), and God has selected (for His purpose) the weak things of the world to shame the things which are strong (revealing their frailty). God has selected (for His purpose) the insignificant (base) things of the world, and the things that are despised and treated with contempt, (even) the things that are nothing, so that He might reduce to nothing the things that are, so that no one may (be able to) boast in the presence of God. But it is from Him that you are in Christ Jesus, who became to us wisdom from God (revealing wisdom from God, revealing His plan of salvation), and righteousness (making us acceptable to God), and sanctification (making us holy and setting us apart for God), and redemption (providing our ransom from the penalty for sin)." 1 Corinthians 1:26-30

About Me

I can't speak on Beautifying Sins when you know little to nothing about me. In case you haven't read my first bestseller Confidence Unlocked, let me properly introduce myself and try to get you caught up the best way I can. Some scenarios from my life I have shared involved confusing infatuation with love. As a matter of fact, I was once desperate to be in love that I tried to force infatuation to evolve into love. I ignored signs and made excuses, insisting that it was love. Accepting and settling for less than I deserved while developing counterproductive characteristics. I did my best to force those who hurt me to love me instead of seeking healing from infatuation. Where and how did this all begin?

Before I knew it, I was toxic overdosing on this drug addiction. It's common to mistake infatuation with love. To be honest with myself, I have to examine whether it was a part of my process or was I just bluntly ignoring the red flags. It's impossible to appreciate the good without experiencing the bad. I could not fully accept the good without healing from my past. At this point in my life, I wanted to be free, beautiful, authentic, refreshed, and rejuvenated. I desire to be in a less chaotic space. Journey with me through the emotional rollercoaster of Beautifying Sins! It's too late to put the book down now. You've already accepted the challenge of beautifying your sins. Our stories may be different but, I'm sure that you will be able to relate. There are some things in my life that I would rather ignore or find an escape from them. But, if I do that, how would I be able to get to this place to tell you how to beautify a sin?

The majority called me Kiwi in school and my neighborhood during my pre-teen and teenage years. During this stage, my life seemed to be on repeat. Tests, trials, and tribulations seemed to be all life had destined for me. My mother raised me, and my father was not present in my life, as I desired him to be. I'm a domestic violence survivor and have struggled with low self-esteem and insecurities. These were the biggest events of my traumatic experiences that resulted in me living my life in formal sin.

As difficult as it may be for one to admit, having emotionally unavailable parents leads to feelings of rejection, withdrawal, immaturity, and self-centeredness. No one wants to admit they need healing, even when they are broken and toxic. Why? We like the protection of the façade. I'm okay. I have to be strong. People who lack accountability and self-awareness often affect their children or mates as much as themselves. That affected child was me!

It seemed like a permanent blemish or stain. I was the child whose behavior began to change. I grew into an emotional, needy teen and adult who longed for the love, security, and affection that I didn't receive as a child. I began searching for healing in all the wrong places. I was unable to start healthy healing without digging deeper into sin. Even though it was painful, I saw myself becoming the same person who hurt me. Committing actions that I knew was wrong and later felt guilty of them. Can you admit your truth? Imagine how hard this was for me to do.

My childhood has affected my adult relationships, some in good and bad ways. In most friendships and relationships, I began to exhibit different traits. I became overly protective and defensive, causing me to struggle with long-term relationships. Excusing inappropriate behavior settling less than I deserved. This resulted in many unstable short-term relationships in which I confused infatuation with love. My emotional neediness, low self-esteem, and fear of abandonment were fueled by my misplaced attachment, lack of self-love, selfishness, substance abuse, physical abuse, and the loss of my faith, hope, and joy.

Being raised by a strong black woman left one of the biggest impacts on me. I grew to be dominant, strong, nurturing, caring, compassionate, independent, and ambitious. But, I also struggled with pride issues. I didn't want the help; I hid my feelings, and I rarely let down my guard.

I'm Bruised

Being raised with an absentee father led to my being an emotional and needy child in search of the attention that I desired from my father. The desire to have an emotional, physical, and mental connection with him grew as I got older. Before I go deeper into this chapter, let me be very clear. An absentee parent is not just being physically absent from a child. It is also being spiritually, mentally, and emotionally unavailable to a child. Children suffer from that lack of emotion, attention, support, and love.

I would spend every other weekend with my dad, but there wasn't much time spent with just him and me. I would either spend time with his girlfriend, whom I truly adored, or get dropped off at his sister's. Most of my weekends with him were spent with my cousins. Because we were close in age, they were more relatable to me than him, but truth be told, that wasn't the way I wanted our relationship to be. Daddy would go out with the guys, leaving me alone with his girlfriend. On Sundays, the basement was for him and all of his boys to watch football. They would fire up the grill, feed me, and send me to my room. During this time alone, my fear of abandonment developed. Although the basement probably wasn't the appropriate setting for a little girl, I still wanted that relationship with my father. After all, there isn't anything wrong with women being into sports. As time progressed, the routine became a norm for me. When I dared to address my concerns, I was told I was being too grown. Eventually, I stopped speaking.

I started to date. I was meeting males from the neighborhood or just hanging out with my friends. Although I had many male "associates", I was unable to commit to any friendship or relationship. Logically, someone suffering from abandonment would seek commitment and continuity, right? Well, not me. I believed if I allowed myself to expect too much from someone, they would abandon me. Thinking it was no point in setting myself up to be hurt, I believed their abandonment was inevitable. I had to guard myself by beating them to the punch. In many of these guarded scenarios, I expressed my love for them, just as Daddy would always tell me that he loved me at the end of my visits or conversations.

No question about it, I knew Daddy loved me. I'm his only child. Because I heard those three words so frequently, I repeated them freely. Eager for a daddy's girl relationship, before you knew it, I was acting just like him or accepting the same traits from the men I chose to date. Being a child, this was the path that I took. As a parent, we are the first person that our children begin to idolize. Growing up with this attitude my actions were not very loyal; I used the word love in the wrong manner. Before I knew it, I was being hurt by love. Even still, I feared intimacy. I was afraid to let my guard down and wouldn't allow anyone to get too close to me.

Entering my sophomore year in high school at the age of fifteen, I finally opened up to someone. Still afraid to get too attached, I began to seem uncaring. I did not want to give him a chance to discover the real me behind the fortifications. I was too immature and toxic to acknowledge the behavior that I was demonstrating. I love you. Those were always the words that Dad and I exchanged. My mother and I seldom exchanged those words; I was more comfortable exchanging the powerful words with a man because that was where I most received them from.

Fear of abandonment has many topics that one can tend to overlook. The "I'm okay. I'm fine. Nothing is wrong." façade seems to be true because we don't really sit and dig into our toxicity. We must uncover the trauma to be able to heal. Instead, we ignore it rather than hold ourselves accountable. The ACCOUNTABILITY that should begin in one's childhood is often hindered by childhood trauma.

What many people consider normal, in all actuality, is not. Bitterness or resentment caused by the death of a loved one, neglect, emotional or physical abuse, and the tension between parents that may keep the child away from one of them is not normal. Yes, death is to be expected, but the other things listed are simply not okay and should not be accepted as normal. Very seldom can parents honestly say they thought about how the experiences with their children were creating insecure attachments or insecurities. I can admit I didn't evaluate myself as a parent until I began writing Beautifying Sins.

I'm bruised because there's been a creation of insecure attachment collectively between the two. You may be curious about what an insecure attachment is. As I sat on my friend's couch one night, he told me how he could see and feel my insecurities behind all the make-up that I had caked on and the clothes I had chosen to wear. My stomach literally dropped when I heard that. It was "Mask Off" season. I still had a layer that I had not even begun to peel off. I tried to bury it and ignore it. I didn't want to reveal it and move forth. It had deep roots.

To sum up defining insecure attachment, from researching various psychology platforms. It is a relationship where the bond is contaminated by fear from mixed emotions, such as dependence and rejection. People with an insecure attachment expect other people to abandon them or harm them in some way. What I just shared sounds crazy, right? Well, I was raised with an insecure attachment. I was intrigued at how this conversation with my friend came about after God told me there was more that needed to be told in this book. Because in that moment, that was me. I was appalled by how necessary that conversation was for me to be transparent and authentic with myself. It revealed the key to unlock a mask that I had never acknowledged existed. I had never had a desire to speak about it. I must be able to identify the cause of my sins to attempt to begin beautifying them. Hopefully, this will inspire you to dig down to your roots. That's usually where it all begins.

    Yes, I respect how my mother raised me, but was that any healthier for me? Then I have a father who I barely understand. As a child, a healthy relationship with both of my parents was what I needed most. That's the thing I kept hidden. When I wanted to speak, I was always taught my opinion or voice didn't matter because I was a child. My parents felt children were being grown when an attempt was made to express themselves.

Honor Thy Father and Mother

"Children, obey your parents in the Lord [that is, accept their guidance and discipline as His representatives], for this is right [for obedience teaches wisdom and self-discipline]. 2Honor [esteem, value as precious] your father and your mother [and be respectful to them]–this is the first commandment with a promise– 3so that it may be well with you, and that you may have a long life on earth. 4Fathers, do not provoke your children to anger [do not exasperate them to the point of resentment with demands that are trivial or unreasonable or humiliating or abusive; nor by showing favoritism or indifference to any of them], but bring them up [tenderly, with lovingkindness] in the discipline and instruction of the Lord." Ephesians 6:1-4 AMP

Since we're talking about sin, I have deeply defined sin at the beginning of our challenge. I have to be open, honest, and transparent with you and not give an image that all was well. Throughout my journey of richly evaluating myself and digging down to the root, I began my healing process. I stumbled across the command "Honor your father and mother" found in many books of the Bible, including Exodus, Leviticus, Proverbs, Colossians, Ephesians, Matthew, and Deuteronomy. Although I was never a problem child who blatantly disobeyed my parents, I found this commandment interesting even after becoming a mother myself.

God knows we, as children, always believe we are right and attempt to figure things out on our own. We also want to be grown and do what we want to do. When we express ourselves, are we being too grown and disobedient? God knows we are human and, at times, incapable of following His commands. The beauty in Christ is that He made a way for us to be forgiven.

Looking at the shattered woman in my mirror, I've realized how my "strength" has harmed me. It added a link to the generational chain on both sides of my family. I acknowledge my dating and relationship problems, pride issues, controlling demeanor, and insecurities. As bad as I wanted to feel fatherly love or experience healthy love in general, I still masked the desire with my strength. I was too strong, independent, dominant, and ambitious. Clinging to unhealthy attachments, insecurities, and fear of abandonment. One of the biggest commandments that I now reflect on is "honor your father and mother". My insecurities often made me unwilling to submit and obey. This command puzzled me because our first significant relationships are generally with our parents.

Through my walk of healing, I've realized how healthy it is to uncover the roots of our pain and weakness. True healing does not result from identifying and assigning guilt but from trusting God. The only way to genuine respect and obedience is forgiveness. I struggled with that one. I could never truly forgive because I couldn't let go. I couldn't let go of the pain I had experienced without clarity. But, I also attempted to mask my pain and keep it moving. In 2017, when I began writing Confidence Unlocked, I was able to face my truths and remove my mask to start my healing. As I said, it is healthy to uncover the roots of your pain and weakness. Don't always bury it and settle into a state of oblivion. You create a bigger issue when you lack self-awareness. I've learned how important it is on this journey to be aware, especially being a mother to an incredible eight-year-old daughter. Parents have to heal, as well as ensure their children are healing, too.

I believe the majority of our trauma, pain, and weaknesses are created in our early childhood. Would you agree? Our parents, Generational X and Baby Boomers, generally ignore their damage or are oblivious to it. They believe these painful occurrences to be the norm and pass their trauma down to the millennials. We then become parents and continue the same cycle for our children, Generational Z. While I didn't necessarily want to be this independent, super strong, "don't let your guard down" kind of woman, I did want to be loved correctly, build trust, and fall safely into the arms of a man who wouldn't intentionally hurt me. Being confused by one and not receiving from the other, I began crying out. Some of my self-destructive behavior was intentional to get the attention of the other. I did not know what else to do. Living with a headstrong, independent mother, the result of my crying out would always be me getting my butt beat. Why? That didn't make it any better. Growing up, it was a little rocky for me to obey, honor, and respect my parents. Of course, our parents base their parenting on how they were taught and raised by their parents.

This was a burden for me! I truly wanted to be both mommy's and daddy's girl. I wanted a balanced, healthy, safe haven for both of my parents to be my best friends. I had so much animosity hidden inside of me that a mask was the best way for me to accept and obey "honor thy father and mother". No, I am not saying you can do and say whatever to your parents, elders, or humanity without any consequences, Generational Z. You should create respectful, healthy relationships and build those relationships on love, trust, discipline, and security – not just cycles, fear, insecurities, and intimidation.

"But to answer your question, you know the commandments: 'You must not commit adultery. You must not murder. You must not steal. You must not testify falsely. Honor your father and mother." Luke 18:20

CONFUSED

Intense emotions, easy to get confused with the two
But differ in their actuality of love, intensity, and outcome
Have you ever been confused between the two, too?
Addictive love, sexual attraction, unreasoning passion or love
Interpersonal love, emotion, feeling of intense affection

Urgency, intensity, abandonment of what was once valued
Like an addictive drug, infatuation gets controlled by the brain
Becoming so caught up, now your heart is left with some sort of a stain
Recklessly committed to satisfy ones all-consuming lust
Ignoring all signs, thinking aloud this just has to be a must
Forcing the feeling for a sexual desire
Possibly thinking there could be some type of healing
Instead emptiness, anxiety, confusion, high-risk choices
Insecurities, wild obsessions, delusional you seem to be
Thinking you're living an all-American dream
It all happened so fast, could it just possibly be?

The power in the first kiss, the touch giving hope of forever
The desire in the eyes, falling for the potential you began to endeavor

Love may be motivation, not realizing lust you're really settling
You mistook their lust for love, so you gave your heart
More so used than adored
Here for the benefits, calls and texts are not limitless
Can you see how it can be easy to conflate the two? Baffling?
I only can imagine you believed I just described love

A slow, deeper approach; craving a connection more than anything
Comfortability, stability, live a life realistically
Faithfulness, loyalty, confidence, sacrifices, commitment, security,
Seems to me something like flourishing
A kiss of confirmation, the touch of no worries, polite assertiveness
One can really get use to this

Hold no grudges, just let it go, brings out understanding and trust
Acceptance of one for them; it's a process there's no rush
Brings you peace, able to provide explanation, very mature grows stronger with friendship
Calm and can heal you, make you a better person, more so partnership
Accountability, settling differences, genuine intentions
Respectful of other's feelings
Non-chaotic, an intense deep affection
That's what I hope to encounter – the true definition of love

Shattered

I looked in the mirror; I swear to you it shattered
Broken glass everywhere
One good piece, I gave it a stare
You see, because this life here is confusing and bruising
No way that God could use me
I'm worthless, not good enough
What possibly could I give to this world?
Looking through my lenses that were only
Shattered

I make "love" to feel loved
I get high to find an escape
I get drunk, so I can't think straight
I wear a mask to keep hidden from my past
I run away from church; they can't relate
I lie to keep from telling the truth
Accountability, please; I love living life on repeat
Let me calm down
This here is getting too deep
I'm Shattered

No lessons or answers
Can you even notice me?
I hold my head down
So, you don't notice my frown

> Pass me your crown
> I need strength when you're not around
> I know you don't even notice me
> Because I'm comfortable living in who I "desire" to be
> Crazy part is that's not even me
> The broken pieces? That's more so Key
> I allow you to see what I want you to see
> And that's not even my true well-being
> I'm Shattered

That was the life I thought was predestined for me. Completely shattered, I felt the broken glass cutting me deep. I realized my flesh was weak. So weak that now I'm oblivious to not acknowledging my true identity. I want to say I was a little grenade! A little toxic bomb who was afraid to change.

It was my story, but I was afraid to face it. How dare I speak aloud about my life. That's no pretty image to paint. It was so embarrassing, humiliating, degrading, hurtful. I was so prideful that I couldn't fathom the words to even begin telling it. I made all kinds of excuses, covered my bruises, wore a smile, remained silent, and masked all my true feelings.

What did I have to offer the world besides guilt, hurt, shame, toxicity, and defeat? There is nothing special about me, I told myself. These were the crazy thoughts I once had about myself. I couldn't understand why God would allow my father not to be present in my life, as I desired him to be. Why was my mother always so hard, disciplining me and teaching me that independence was vital? Why would He allow me to feel that I was worthless? Why would He allow me to have low self-esteem, thinking I was not beautiful enough or good enough? Why would I have to endure domestic violence? Why would I be placed in the situation to possibly be labeled a felon? How could He allow me to become pregnant by my abuser? Why wasn't the trigger just pulled and my life taken with the bullet? Why must my heart be broken repeatedly and hurt by so many? Why did I have to be counted among the single parents? Why does life seem so hard? I'm barely able to make ends meet. Why can't I even keep hold of myself? Everyone says, "Jesus loves you," but it seems as if He's forgotten all about me. Can you keep it real and accept this challenge along with me? I'm still looking in my mirror and constantly seeing my broken pieces!

"He taught me and said to me, '' Let your heart hold fast my words; keep my commandments and live. 5Get (skillful and godly) wisdom! Acquire understanding (actively seek spiritual discernment, mature comprehension, and logical interpretation)! Do not forget nor turn away from the words of my mouth." Proverbs 4:4-5

Processing

    I feel the stabbing of my back and the heat rising from my feet. My tears are overflowing, my voice is gone, and I can barely speak. I can't hold my head high. I feel the critics critiquing me. My vision is blurred, and my soul is on fire. I feel like my life is at a standstill.

    While tossing and turning, sweating, and barely able to breathe, I cry out, "Oh God, what is happening to me? Help me! Heal my father! Help him notice me; help him fill the gap. Show him how I desire him to be. Take away the footsteps that I'm now following from my past." I screamed this aloud from my room. It was a repetitive prayer.

    Every time I would ask, He would always reply, "No, not yet, my daughter. If I allowed him to notice you now, you wouldn't be able to handle him ignoring you again."

"But, Father, that's my father!" I cried out. "How could my own father forsake me?" I asked.

"My daughter, not yet. You're not ready to accept that kind of test," He told me. It was His last response.

Instantly, bursting into tears and confused, I would cry out, "I'm not ready to accept that kind of test? Why do I feel like I am being ignored by my own father, the man who helped create me?"

Still, the only answer I would get was, "Not yet." I never could understand why that was all God would ever say and expect me to be still. I grew frustrated watching my friends have great father and daughter relationships while mine was broken. The feeling that my dad didn't love me was almost unbearable. How cruel of you, I always thought. My hurt overpowered me, but I masked my pain, pretending everything was okay. I expected results, a change, and answers instantly, but I got none. Instead, I was left wondering, "How can I get Dad to notice me?"

I was attention-seeking! It was very cliché and immature of me. I lied to my father about something so silly. I could have told him the truth, but I chose to lie. He eventually found out I was lying. I can't recall how he learned the truth, but wow! Dad was finally there for me. Even amid my wrongdoing, he was there. He was right there yelling and screaming, "Go get the belt!" That's what he instructed me to do. He spanked me powerfully while my tears were steady flowing. As bad as it hurt, I was actually happy. As crazy as it sounds, I had some time to be with my father. Sadly, shortly after, he grabbed his cigarettes and retreated to the basement. Although I was dead wrong, I wanted him to be there to console me after my wrongdoing. Again, my fear of abandonment returned.

Slamming my door, I cried out, "God, what else do I need to do so my father will notice me? I hate it here! Does my father not love me?"

"My daughter, not yet," He repeated yet again.

It was normal for me to act out and receive a beating from my mother, but my father's reaction completely shocked me. Not making an excuse to justify my actions that resulted in punishment, but by uncovering my roots, I discovered a pattern.

I felt I had to act out to get his attention. I did what I had to do so my mother would have enough and be forced to call my father. My goal was for her to tell him, "Come get your daughter." Let's just say I learned my lesson. I never lied to my dad again, but the time I spent was either with his girlfriend, sister, or niece. Very seldom did he and I spend any quality time bonding.

Again, I called on the Lord, but he would still reply, "Not yet, my daughter. If I allow him to notice you the way you desire, you won't notice me. If I grant you what you ask right now, there would be no need for me. There would be no need for me in your family. There's a need for your private sufferings for the world to see all in its right timing."

Not understanding any of this, I was living my life on the edge. I began displaying my toxic traits to fill a void, as well as to escape. I began doing it in most, if not all, of my relationships. Insecure, wanting attention, using sex, and starting arguments just because. I'm curious. Am I the only one who did that?

In the blink of an eye, I remember having a pistol in my face. God, why me? Why do I have to endure pain to feel that I am loved? Why do I have to lower myself to see the good in him? Why didn't he just pull the trigger and kill me? That sure would've relieved me from all that I'm feeling. When will I be able to endure a real, genuine relationship? These were some of the questions I asked God.

Once more, He replied, "Not yet, Daughter. If I grant you your wish, you won't be able to experience a God-ordained relationship. You won't know what it feels like to be loved the right way. You won't know what it's like to be loved without the pain."

I felt I was getting closer to God, but still, during my agony and pain, He always told me, "Not yet." That is not the response I wanted to hear in my time of need, though. What worked best for me? Still ignoring my guilt. I used toxic addictions to numb my pain momentarily.

It felt as though I was getting thrown into the fiery pit of hell every time I was living a life that was best for me. Thinking aloud, I asked, "God, are you punishing me? Do you not love me? Why is this happening to me?"

"No, I am not punishing you," He assured me.

Spiritual discernment, mature comprehension, logical interpretation, and Godly wisdom were the main keys I lacked. It's the reason nothing made sense to me, and I believed that God was punishing me.

"For I know the plans and thoughts that I have for you," says the Lord, "plans for peace and well-being and not for disaster, to give you a future and a hope. 12Then you will call on Me and you will come and pray to Me, and I will hear [your voice] and I will listen to you. 13Then [with a deep longing] you will seek Me and require Me [as a vital necessity] and [you will] find Me when you search for Me with all your heart. 14I will be found by you," says the Lord, "and I will restore your fortunes and I will [free you and] gather you from all the nations and from all the places where I have driven you," says the Lord, "and I will bring you back to the place from where I sent you into exile." Jeremiah 29:11-14

Lost

"Not yet, Daughter, you are still too weak. No. Not yet, Daughter. You wouldn't be able to handle the outcome of that situation. No, not yet. You have to build a little more strength. No, not yet. You still don't know who you are. No, not yet, my child. You are still a child in your walk. No, not yet. You haven't desperately, wholeheartedly searched for me. No, not yet, my daughter. You would not appreciate my grace."

No, not yet, Daughter. I am tired of hearing You say I am lost! If not now, then when? What must I do for You to say when?

Can you relate and admit you've felt the same way? Constantly throwing questions at God, expecting Him to move, but you aren't allowing Him to move through you?

When tribulations happen, do you desire a change? But, instead of a change, something happens again, and you cope in a sinful way that keeps you in a comfort zone. Afraid of growth, you become accustomed to the repetition, thinking you don't need anyone, especially Christ. You have settled into a toxic, sinful, destructive cycle!

What we fail to realize is that what we have accepted as "ordinary" or the norm is a curse. The damaging behavior becomes an addiction we can't function without. It does nothing but boost our ego and rid us of much-needed conviction. This is how we convince ourselves that we're doing nothing wrong and our guilt quickly begins to fade. We don't evaluate ourselves and look at our actions as a sin; we believe our lifestyle is the norm. The enemy plays with our minds and keeps us captive in sin. This is why I am certain many believe one may not be a sinner.

When I hung out with my friends, I was comfortable with living my life within their context. If they were smoking or drinking, then I was comfortable with bypassing my limits to smoke and drink. Committing to actions that I later felt guilty about. This behavior was the greatest defect in my character. We settle into our sinful actions because we're immune to its normality. I still don't understand how some of God's greatest blessings are blessings in disguise. I ran away from those I viewed as a challenge but gravitated to the people who fit my past.

Silly of me, it was me maintaining a "lost" mentality. As I wrote this, tears filled my eyes. John 16:33 suddenly fell in my spirit. "I have told you these things, so that in me you may have peace. In this world you will have trouble. But take heart! I have overcome the world.

"Crying out, I said, "But, God, I'm not at peace."

He gently responded, "You're not in me."

I realized I was not totally at peace, but I was in my process. I was still on my journey to be fully dedicated and committed to God. I was trying, but the road was hard, challenging, and lonely. We get defeated and hopeless because we try to put a period where God only has a comma in our life stories. We become so selfish and react in the flesh, not taking into consideration that Jesus remained sinless while enduring more than our earthly troubles. But, still, we sin. How can one desire to be like Christ without going through some struggles ourselves? God's promise doesn't end with trouble! Moving forward, let's not be quick to put a period where God placed a comma. I know it may become troubling, but you can do it!

Constantly replaying my childhood in my mind kept me captive. It kept me with a lost mentality. I continued to act out, using the excuse of being lost because the melody was on repeat in my mind. Whether we have a positive or negative outlook on life or our struggles, what our mind or thoughts obsess over triggers our behavior. If we don't brush off unwanted thoughts as unfavorable and acknowledge their toxicity and sinfulness, we lack accountability.

Some of God's blessings can be as simple and straightforward as having the capability to lift and raise our hands. Others can be more difficult to discern, like the blessing of brokenness. I know you are probably thinking, how in the world is there a blessing in being broken? Look at me now! I am so blessed to have been gracefully broken because now, I am able to share my story.

God's blessing isn't always materialistic. There is a blessing in learning and being positioned to be able to give wisdom. We receive bigger blessings once we adjust our lens and realize we have to go through lost seasons of life to be blessed to bless others. The biggest blessing is this thing called GRACE!

"I will make you into a great nation, and I will bless you and make you famous, and you will be a blessing to others. 3I will bless those who bless you and curse those who treat you with contempt. All the families on earth will be blessed through you." Genesis 12:2-

Not Ordinary

Not yet,
I'm curious is this some kind of test
A test that seems as if I'm only failing
But it's making me really upset
Ignoring my pain
God, this can't be your plan
You only keep telling me, "No, not yet"
All because I'm
Not Ordinary

But, I'm not understanding
I'm lost and confused
What is it about my life that you're deciding to choose?
You say I'm not ordinary
Just how would I be ordinary?
Your pain has to empower you
So that you'll be able to inspire, too
I don't just say, "No, not yet," to punish you
But to reward you of deserving your crown
Because you're
Not Ordinary

Cleansing

"Let us go right into the presence of God with sincere hearts fully trusting Him. For our guilty consciences have been sprinkled with Christ's blood to make us clean, and our bodies have been washed with pure water." Hebrews 10:22

You have to examine the areas of your life where you are not honest with yourself. These are the areas where who you are and how you think, act, and feel don't align. This realization is the beginning of spiritual cleansing, and that's where I was, too! Acknowledging my inconsistencies gave me the ability to start listening more to my heart than my mind. I began to remove the blockage that inhibited my natural growth. I had to admit my thoughts, feelings, desires, and even some of my actions were getting in the way. I identified physical issues, mental blocks, and the tension in my mind, fear, anxiety, and ego as hindrances.

If you are not a spiritual or religious person, feel free to call this stage in your journey energy cleansing. This type of healing seeks to identify and cure any problem that is manifesting in our lives. Many believe in crystals, sage, and CBD, not realizing they are looking for God while choosing to idolize Him in material things.

Cleansing is based on energy, and our energy during tests, trials, and tribulations impacts the outcome. I know you may be thinking, where is she going with this? She sounds crazy.

I thought I had successfully dealt with my emotional trauma, but I had not. I still experienced recurring physical, mental, emotional, and even some spiritual problems. The negative energy was still there. It still impacted me. It was bothersome, and I still carried the negative energy from my past.

I learned in my cleansing season that once I put my pride to the side and acknowledged my toxic ways, I was finally taking full responsibility. It then became an easier process to remove and release the negativity that was keeping me in bondage.

After a difficult emotional encounter, have you ever felt a heaviness? You know how we say "Good Vibes Only"? Well, we pick up and carry negative vibes from others. The way we respond to it affects us, too. If we feed into the negativity, it is more likely to become a part of us.

Do you believe you are harboring negative energy? If so, when? What do you?

_____
_____
_____
_____
_____

It is so easy to say, "Get rid of the source and heal from it!" However, it's definitely a process to execute. How exactly do you rid yourself of the source if the source is a parent, family member, or someone to whom you are attached until death do you part? I struggled with this, too. I knew a lot of my stubborn, toxic ways came from childhood trauma, but it was time for me to take responsibility for my actions instead of using my childhood as an excuse. Here's how I began to do it. I hope it will help you, too.

Approach the process with a positive, upbeat attitude that will nourish instead of captivating you. Cleansing releases the heavy, distorted energy that you constantly carry.

Let me be clear. Cleansing is not a one-time event. It is indeed a PROCESS! I realized the importance of cleansing when I began to dim my own light. Constantly feeling fatigued, lack of motivation, even losing interest in things I thoroughly enjoyed were signs I needed a cleanse. My dull energy was becoming transferable and affecting my daughter, coworkers, and anyone with whom I had contact. My energy caused me to no longer be into the person I was dating. I was insensitive to my energy. When I received what I gave, I disliked it and wanted no parts of it. That often happens. The blockage we carry within becomes hard for us to see.

Detoxify your mental and emotional state of mind.

I know you are probably thinking, How in the hell do you do that? You have to realize how your mental and emotional state of mind controls your life story. Detoxification releases old hurt and prepares you for new goals. Publishing my first book, Confidence Unlocked, was a detox for me. I was able to release all that had hurt me. By speaking my truth and removing my mask, I was able to stop pretending to be someone that wasn't even me. It was a step in freeing myself from my negative past.

Don't be afraid to seek help. Self-help may not work for everyone. Find you a Pastor, therapist, life coach, or trusted friend who doesn't sugarcoat anything with you. ACCOUNTABILITY!

I had barricaded my heart with resentment, bitterness, rage, immorality, anxiety, fear, bondage, infidelity, deception, addictions, jealousy, depression, etc. before beginning to be cleansed from them all. I had my moments when I needed to go deeper and cleanse my heart with faith.

"Wash me clean from my guilt. Purify me from my sin. 3For I recognized my rebellion; it haunts me day and night." Psalm 51:2-3

Repentance

"People who conceal their sins will not prosper, but if they confess and turn from them, they will receive mercy." Proverbs 28:13

Before I go into the next chapter, Repentance, remember this journey never ends. You may be thinking, Well, I cleansed my sin, so that's the way to beautify a sin, right? WRONG! To me, a better definition of cleansing would be identifying and being accountable, while repentance is regret, remorse, confession, and change. Just because we took the time to identify and cleanse our sin doesn't mean we've made our sins beautiful.

Repentance is the progression of having peace of mind, comfort, and joy. It is not just asking for forgiveness, but there has to be a change as a person. The path you are traveling has to change. Truths have to be faced and accountability taken. There is a PROCESS to becoming a BETTER person. Surrendering your life, your plans, and your ways to the One who has more in store for you than you can ever imagine are all part of repentance.

Going back to the beginning of our challenge, I asked, "Why do you sin?" If I had asked you to send your answers, I could only imagine what a lot of you may have said. I'm sure many would say, "I'm not sure," "It's a comfort zone," "It's pleasurable", or simply "I don't sin." To be fair and answer the question myself, I would have to say sin was simply a safe place for me. As I said before, it was an escape to avoid facing my truths and becoming a better person. I preferred to remain a broken, shattered, confused, lost, and bruised person because that was all I knew! I was childish and immature, with no discernment or Godly wisdom. Although it hurt me, felt guilty, and I was accustomed to it. My sin was the norm. I had no accountability, no inspiration, and no one around who fit my future – only my present and past. Growing, healing, cleansing, evolving, and repenting hurts; it does not always feel good. It's not a walk in the park. Change takes hard, dedicated, committed work, but it is well worth it.

I sat back and reflected on Proverbs 28:13-14: "People who conceal their sins will not prosper, but if they confess and turn from them, they will receive mercy. Blessed are those who fear to do wrong, but the stubborn are headed for serious calamities." I think to myself, WOW! This is the truth! I was stuck. There was no growth in me as long as I concealed my sins. As soon as I began to confess, turn from them, and feared the same, I began to desperately, wholeheartedly seek God, and here I am today.

Are you ready to begin your journey of repentance? Why or why not?
_____
_____
_____
_____
_____

"I don't really understand myself, for I want to do what is right, but I don't do it. Instead, I do what I hate. 16But if I know that what I am doing is wrong, this shows that I agree that the law is good. 17So I am not the one doing wrong; it is sin living in me that does it. 18And I know that nothing good lives in me, that is, in my sinful nature. I want to do what is right, but I can't. 19I want to do what is good, but I don't. I don't want to do what is wrong, but I do it anyway. 20But if I do what I don't want to do, I am not really the one doing wrong; it is sin living in me that does it. 21I have discovered this principle of life—that when I want to do what is right, I inevitably do what is wrong. 22I love God's law with all my heart. 23But there is another power within me that is at war with my mind. This power makes me a slave to the sin that is still within me. 24Oh, what a miserable person I am! Who will

free me from this life that is dominated by sin and death? 25Thank God! The answer is in Jesus Christ our Lord. So you see how it is: In my mind I really want to obey God's law, but because of my sinful nature I am a slave to sin." Romans 7:15-25

The hardest part of this journey for me, honestly, is forgiveness. Without me being able to forgive, it's difficult for me to let go. That's my biggest issue! I keep trying to forgive him, but I just can't let it go. I forgave them, but I am still angry about what they did. I realized how holding on to my past hurt was causing me bitterness and keeping me from receiving my blessings. I can't change what happened in my past, but I can control my present and change my response for a better impact on my future.

Without full forgiveness and repentance, I lived my life prideful, which led to destruction and animosity, leaving the door wide open for sin. I had to repent in order to break this destructive cycle of behavior and patterns. Repentance is telling God that I need help to change my thinking, attitude, and behavior.

Realizing I can't forgive without repentance, I forgave with a scorned heart. I forgave out of hatred and bitterness, knowing deep down that I was unable to let go. Was I really forgiving, though? On my journey to beautifying sins, I've realized my maturity, growth, connection, discernment, wisdom, and relationship with Christ, and I'm destined to see us all win together. No, I am not perfect, but my goal is to become better, and my faith has secured my future.

Be honest and transparent with yourself. Think of what in your life needs to be changed, repented. Write it out. There's a difference in being visual and keeping the thought captive in your head. There is more accountability and responsibility in seeing your goal for personal growth.

_____
_____
_____
_____
_____
_____
_____
_____
_____
_____

Beautifully Free

"But he did not doubt or waver in unbelief concerning the promise of God, but he grew strong and empowered by faith, giving glory to God, 21being fully convinced that God had the power to do what He had promised." Romans 4:20-21

Taking accountability can become overwhelming, and that's where I was. I was beyond overwhelmed and stressed out, wanting to be free while failing to realize I was already free. One thing's for sure; my faith has never wavered through this. I know you may be thinking, Well, Key, how can you say that you are free? What drastically changed in just one chapter?

It has been longer than just one chapter. The time has extended further than just a chapter. This chapter, my journey, began in 2017. Along the way, and because of my immature mentality, it seemed crazy to me how life works.

The way we think and how we allow our thoughts to captivate us is what messes us up. Living in your mind instead of your heart is one dangerous place to be. Our mind doesn't speak from love. Negative thoughts easily captivate us and have us believing they are our reality. When we speak and live from our minds, we're speaking and living in dysfunction. Most of the time, the dysfunction is from what we were taught or what we've seen or felt. That's what takes root in us. When a storm comes, we are afraid and react in a dysfunctional manner because that is what we know best.

We speak and live in what we accept as customary. I'm sure you've heard many say, "Listen to or follow your heart." Our heart is a heart for a reason. No matter how hurt, shattered, bruised, confused, or lost we may be, we all want to feel loved. We want to be loved, or we want to give love. Remaining attached to or surrounding ourselves with people who are broken and shattered will make us believe we are still broken, too. That was me, but now I'm beautifully free.

It drastically weighed me down that I still did not have a relationship with my father. Furthermore, after releasing Confidence Unlocked, not having any communication or support from my dad broke me. The hardest thing I have ever had to do was accept this, forgive him, and let it go. The longer I stayed captive in my negative thoughts instead of cleansing and repenting, the longer I remained in the shadow. I continued to struggle and battle in brokenness, becoming gullible to sin.

I will be one that will always tell you that healing and growing hurts. It is an uncomfortable feeling, but do you know why? You are probably thinking, Girl, you just said healing and growing hurts. You've repeated it a few times in this book. Why in the hell would I want to begin to heal and grow? The difference is repentance is not a repetitive broken cycle. Repentance is a change. It's not the norm; it's not customary. It requires you to step out of your comfort zone. It's you growing out of the bondage of your hurt and being uncomfortable with going right back to what hurt you. Yes, the process hurts, but it strengthens you, encourages you, motivates you, inspires you, and empowers you. It's you climbing up the stairs rather than running around in circles. It's stepping out on faith and experiencing something that was never properly introduced to you. Once you have built that strength, you begin to live a happier life!

We're so accustomed to the pain that we fear being beautifully free. We're afraid of self-esteem, self-growth, and being fearless. That's why I love Brandy's song "Scared of Beautiful" written by Frank Ocean: "No wonder why there's no mirrors on these walls no more. You can't tell me why you're so terrified of beautiful, scared of the good more than the evil, scared of the light more than the dark, scared of a truth so much more than a lie. I'm scared for me; I'm scared of me, scared of beautiful."

Why are we so afraid of being beautiful? Why are we scared of being the best version of ourselves? Why are you scared of you? What makes you fearful of change? Why are we afraid of the unfamiliarity?

We want it so bad but, we're afraid of its unfamiliarity. Growing and healing "glowing" is a commitment to changing for the better because you want better. That's what and who you are created to be. You want to flourish and prosper beautifully free. It's a journey; it's a process. It does not end until our Father says, " My child, well done, my good and faithful servant."

I've learned that it may hurt others once you begin to use your voice and share your story. Do it anyway! You will lose some friends and your circle will become smaller, grow anyway! If you allow yourself to stay mute because of fear and mask your voice, you're not doing anything but hurting yourself. You are not hurting anyone else. You are satisfying their sinful ways instead of beautifying your sins because you're committing to staying the same, what's normal, and familiar to you.

I'm able to be beautifully free, and I desire to Empower Too Inspire you to be beautifully free, too! I follow my heart rather than my mind. My mind is a collection of reminders of what and who hurt me. I instantly think everything and everyone is going to do the same. When following my mind, I believe everyone is going to abandon me or hurt me as soon as I get attached. I think everyone is going to abuse me when I am crying out for love or help regardless of what their actions say. I'm beautifully free because I've acknowledged, taken responsibility, and have complete remorse for living in my thoughts and my mind. I'm beautifully free because I am FULLY aware I couldn't – and still can't – be on this journey on my own. I'm beautifully free because I put my trust and faith in Him, and in Christ, there's freedom. Left to my own devices, I would have remained the toxic, broken, bitter, shattered, confused, lost Kiawana, but I had to step up my faith. I believed the Holy Spirit would free me from my thoughts. I'm beautifully free because I have committed to growing, glowing, evolving, and changing even when it hurts me. I'm beautifully free because I desire to be a better woman, mother, and wife. I want to be an inspiration, encouragement, and an example for myself and my daughter, if no one else. I'm beautifully free because I'm a warrior, and generational curses end with me. I'm beautifully free because I know it will happen for me.

    I'm beautifully free because my faith secures me. I'm beautifully free because, in the midst of a storm, I don't allow negative thoughts to captivate me. Instead, I release them. I'm beautifully free because that's what God has destined for me. I'm beautifully free because I learned to truly love, forgive, and accept myself and others, just as God has done for me. I'm beautifully free because I learned to love many wherever they are on their journey, just as Christ has done with me. I'm beautifully free because I made up my mind to accept, forgive, and release all the pain that others may have caused me. I'm beautifully free because that's how I chose to be.

I beautified my sins by choosing to repent and commit to Christ! I beautified my sins by being beautifully free. Are you ready to beautify your sins, too?

Acceptance Is Freedom
"Allow Your Weakness to Guide You to Your Freedom"

I know we are all very familiar with the scripture "Faith without works is dead," right? This, indeed, has been the realest statement for me throughout my season of growth and maturity. Why? Yes, I told you that I am beautifully free by choosing to be committed to growing, glowing, evolving, and changing even when it hurts me, But how will my words match my actions? Just how and where exactly did I begin?

Sitting back, I always thought to myself, how can I speak to others when my home is not in order? I still had the desire to mend the relationship between my father and me. I recall meeting Linda Clemons at a conference. Instantly, she said to me, "When you love, you love hard. But when you get hurt, you hurt, and it is hard for you to let go." That is, by far, one of my biggest weaknesses. I love too hard, but how in the world did this woman know?

The following day, I ran into Mrs. Clemons again. I revisited her comment from the day before. She told me, "The hardest thing for you to do is to forgive and let go." My mind was running everywhere. I stood there in amazement because I couldn't even hide it. It is so hard for me to forgive and let go.

Not only did I struggle with forgiving my father, but also with many others along the way who hurt me. It had been hard to forgive and let go, especially with my daughter's father. How do you expect to heal, if you are unable to forgive and let go. As I went deeper with connecting to God, Hebrews 12:14-15 weighed heavy on my heart: Make every effort to live in peace with everyone and to be holy; without holiness no one will see the Lord. See to it that no one falls short of the grace of God and that no bitter root grows up to cause trouble and defile many. It was challenging, but I could not inspire, encourage, or embrace others while wearing a mask myself.

Talk about accountability! I knew I had to make some tough changes and adjustments in my life once this scripture fell in my spirit. I knew God was calling me to a higher place, but a lot of heavy baggage had weighed me down. Because of that baggage, I had been unable to reach all that God had destined for me. I was not living my life in peace, but instead still bore some bitterness and animosity. I was taking on many responsibilities of others that I needed to release.

To be honest, this was a battle for me. Why? Because of my ego. As badly as I wanted to be free from my pride, it had one of the strongest holds on me. When I finally had enough, I had to conquer two of my biggest weaknesses: communication and expressing myself.

In many cases, I was always Key, the builder upper, the one making things right. I initiated conversations or outings to mend broken issues. I was fed up with doing that. Why is it always Kiawana? I constantly thought. That question repeatedly filled my head. I'm sick of it always being me. The more I allowed this thought into my head, the angrier I became.

I went deeper into prayer, being strategic with my request:

Father,

Parenting is humbling. We, as parents, feel helpless to our faults. We know we won't get it right every time, but our pride can be our own worst enemy. Many times our patience runs out, and our choices don't always align with Your will. Father, I am guilty of this myself, but I ask for Your forgiveness. I ask for Your forgiveness for myself, my mother, my father, and anyone else who may have hurt me in the past that I have decided to bury with some form of toxic addiction, better known as sin. God, we fall short as parents. I have made plenty of mistakes while parenting. I ask that You bless the generations that have gone before me, the legacies and lessons they left for me and after me. I pray that You break the generational chains of all that wasn't taught well or the right way. Help me to honor my parents. Have Your way and perform a miracle in my heart so that I can forgive those who have mistreated, oppressed, and abused me. God, I can't do it in my power alone. My power leads to anger, resentment, and animosity. So first help me be able to forgive myself. Heavenly Father, adjust my perspective daily to see others as You see them and to honor the people You have placed in my life. Forgive me for criticizing my parents, battling them, and dishonoring them with my words or behavior, whether I was right or wrong. Help not just me, Father, but all to honor You by how we honor others. I thank You for making a way for me even when I fall short and don't deserve it. Your love is forever. There's greater power in Your name, and here I am now calling You to give me the strength that I need to make it through. I can't make it on my own, but I sincerely desire to be free. Help me to be able to accept the response that I may get from You, whether or not it's the one I may want. Give me peace and closure, even if the response is not what I desire to hear. Let me not have expectations, Father, but acceptance to love and meet people where they are and where I wish for them to be. I'm calling on you and needing You, God.

> *Love forever and always,*
> *Your daughter, Kiawana*

I committed to fasting and praying, cleansing my spirit so God would be able to use me. I prayed I would be open and not of self in the flesh, but Him in the spirit. I asked myself the famous saying, "What Would Jesus Do?" I had to take my flesh and feelings out of it, thinking only of my purpose. It sounds so easy, but in all actuality, it was the hardest thing for me to do. I just couldn't let go. With Hebrews 12 constantly ringing in my head, I became fearful not to move. It seemed as if the scripture was haunting me.

I had the urge to end the animosity between my father and me. That's where a lot of my holding on to things first began. I had to create peace between the two of us to be able to let go of all that I had been withholding. I just knew if I accepted the response from him, I would be able to let go of everything that had hurt me in my past. It was so easy to say but still so hard for me to do. I feared I wouldn't be able to accept the response he would give me. I had expectations rather than acceptance. Still, with Hebrews 12 reminding me of God's word, I took this burden to God in confidence, knowing He understood the difficulty I was facing and that He is faithful.

Throughout this journey, I strengthened my faith and belief in Christ, knowing I couldn't get to this place on my own. I stopped pointing fingers and started embracing God's command to honor each other. I'm now able to honor family in the same reflection of how Christ loves us. Despite us being dysfunctional and broken, He loves us, and for me to walk in the image of Christ, I must do the same. I honor my parents by releasing judgement for how I've felt about their actions to God, who defends and protects us with mercy and compassion. I couldn't do any of this alone. I needed the strength of God to carry me through.

One evening, I invited my father out to dinner, with no expectations but acceptance. I put my complete faith and trust in God to get me to a place of freedom from the burden that had been weighing me down regardless of the response I received. I had grown to realize that acceptance and accountability were the tools for my freedom. I had allowed my weakness to guide me to my freedom. I value the meaning of letting go and putting me first. I matured in my walk to forgive others as Christ had forgiven me and extended me with grace, even when I least deserve it.

As I continue my walk with Christ and Empower Too Inspire others, I'm constantly reminded to "make every effort to live in peace with everyone and to be holy; without holiness no one will see the Lord." Regardless of how bad a situation may hurt me, I am growing and learning to put my confidence, trust, and faith in Him to release any resentment. I put myself in others' shoes and imagine I am them. God is my example. If I were to turn my back or close the door on them, how would I feel in their shoes? I am beginning to view others as Christ has viewed me in the midst of my mess. I've learned to love others from a distance, lift them in prayer, and allow God to handle the rest instead of talking down on them or cursing them. I am no longer always attempting to mend the broken pieces, thereby overwhelming myself and carrying the burden by holding on to the broken pieces. I value loving others just as Christ has loved me because it creates so much peace for me. I can have all of the faith, hope, and peace in my mind, but if I do not have love in my heart, I have nothing. I don't desire to have a love defined with pain but rather genuine love within my heart.

"Love is patient and kind. Love is not jealous or boastful or proud or rude. 5It does not demand its own way. It is not irritable, and it keeps no record of being wronged. It does not rejoice about injustice but rejoices whenever the truth wins out. Love never gives up, never loses faith, is always hopeful, and endures through every circumstance... 11When I was a child, I spoke and thought and reasoned as a child. But when I grew up, I put away childish things. 12Now we see things imperfectly, like puzzling reflections in a mirror, but then we will see everything with perfect clarity. All that I know now is partial and incomplete, but then I will know everything completely, just as God now knows me completely. 13Three things will last forever---faith, hope, and love---and the greatest of these is love." 1 Corinthians 13:4-5, 11-13

As I sit back and reflect on this passage during my walk in Christ, I can honestly say I am grown, but my actions have been very childish. Due to my childish mentality, I see how I caused many of my broken pieces. Not seeing myself how God sees me resulted in me living my life repeating my sins. I wondered why I always felt incomplete, depressed, sad, alone, lost, and shattered. I had all the hope and faith for a change, but I had no love in my heart. I carried animosity and bitterness. What I defined as love was unhealthy, lies, and broken promises that created the shattered pieces in the mirror.

Beautifying Sins

"The Lord isn't really being slow about His promise, as some people think. No, He is being patient for your sake. He does not want anyone to be destroyed but wants everyone to repent." 2 Peter 3:9

Through my life's calamities, I felt God had forgotten about me. Through my journey of growth, I've realized I have been defining and acting in love the way it was taught, shown to me, and the best way that I've known how. I repeatedly asked God when, and He would always reply, "Not yet." I now finally understand. Back then, I wasn't ready to understand why or when. What makes you say that, Key, you ask? Well, I was childish and never desired to beautify my sins or to mature in my walk with Christ. I now understand why God always told me not yet. He was patient for my sake. He does not want anyone to be destroyed but wants everyone to REPENT!

God, when will I get a break? When will I be free? When will my broken pieces be mended together? When will I find peace, love, joy, hope, and comfort? When will the chaos cease? I remember asking God all of these questions when it seemed everyone was being chosen except me. I'm jubilant when it comes to everyone else's celebration, but I never stopped to look within myself. I could not see that God was trying to get my attention for me to enjoy my celebration. I was so worried about why and when, I didn't notice God was asking me the same thing.

Had I have been more mature in my walk, I would have been able to pay closer attention to His word in Jeremiah 29:11. "For I know the plans and thoughts that I have for you," says the Lord, "plans for peace and well-being and not for disaster, to give you a future and a hope." The season of my calamities and what seemed like chaos in my life was all part of God's plan to use me for His purpose. It's not the end. God is not placing a period in your life, but He is challenging you to grow stronger and closer to Him even when it hurts. No plan will work without Him in it. I'm guilty of this action right along with you. I made decisions and choices on my own, believing I had it all together and would be able to make it through the way I thought was best for me. That was silly of me. I needed God to carry me through. There was no way to carry all of that weight on my own.

"Cry for help, but will anyone answer you? Which of the angels will help you? 2Surely resentment destroys the fool, and jealousy kills the simple. 3I have seen that fool may be successful for the moment, but then comes sudden disaster." Job 5:1-3

As I typed this scripture, tears instantly began streaming down my face. Reflecting, I remember how grateful I am for God's grace and mercy! I recall at a young age crying out for help while lying in the middle of my bedroom floor. No one was there to answer my call, wipe my tears, pick me up off the floor, or reassure me that everything would be okay. I know the feeling of abandonment. I know what it is like to be lost and alone in the midst of your weakest, darkest moment, feeling like you are completely being ignored. But, actually, you are ignoring your own call. The only answer I was able to get from God was, "Not yet." This added more issues for me and caused anxiety. I felt as if I was hallucinating. I was trying to figure out if I was speaking to myself or really hearing from God. I know what it's like receiving an answer you don't want to hear. In the midst of turbulence, the answer sometimes frustrates more than helps you. I know what it's like to look at others and believe it should be you standing there celebrating their success, but instead, you're shattered, lost, bruised, and confused. I know what it's like to carry bitterness and resentment in my heart. I looked back on how I was once the fool. The Lord isn't being slow about His promise, as some people think. No, He is being patient for your sake.

I've allowed my anger, disobedience, guilt, and resentment to destroy me mentally, physically, and emotionally, causing depression, anxiety, and suicidal thoughts. I believed life wasn't for me and wanted the pain to end more than anything. I didn't realize I had to experience that pain to appreciate pure happiness, joy, and love. Many jealous moments allowed me to be simple-minded, failing to see how many lived a life to be loved, noticed, liked, and furthermore, merely for entertainment on social media and they themselves not even knowing their true identity. I was oblivious to the mask that many were wearing, so I found myself feeling envious at times. I was not just jealous of strangers but family and friends, also. I thought, How? Why not me? When will my time come? Judging from the outside image unsure of what's going on within. Can you admit that you've had this same feeling before?

I've experienced many successful moments that suddenly turned into a disaster. When I attempted to take matters into my own hands to fix many situations, it always ended in failure. Staying in toxic situations, believing in the potential that I saw in others, and ignoring my pain only resulted in failure and Kiawana walking away with a broken heart. Reflecting on this passage reminded me even more to give God glory for His grace, mercy, and the way He has restored me. Instead of dealing with many issues, I made the decision to be delivered from them. Instead of learning to cope, I have matured and changed my behavior. I can't take any credit for this, because I am fully aware that I wouldn't be the woman who I am today without God, who is my Lord and Savior. Instead of just reaping, I began repenting.

"People are born for trouble as readily as sparks fly up from a fire. 8If I were you, I would go to God and present my case to Him. 9He does great things too marvelous to understand. He performs countless miracles. 10He gives rain for the earth and water for the fields. 11He gives prosperity to the poor and protects those who suffer. 12He frustrates the plans of schemers so the work of their hands will not succeed." Job 5:7-12

As crazy as it may sound, God already knows we are going to get into some trouble or conflict in life. It is already destined and planned for us. How we respond to our problems is what makes all the difference. How are you posturing yourself through your trouble or conflict in life? Look at me as an example. I suggest you cast all your matters and issues on God. Everything! Don't move until you heal and mature internally. Don't shift your position until your heart changes, and you repent and are delivered.

"But consider the joy of those corrected by God! Do not despise the discipline of the Almighty when you sin. 18For though He wounds, He also bandages. He strikes, but His hands also heal. 19From six disasters he will rescue you; even in the seventh, He will keep you from evil. 20He will save you from death in times of famine, from the power of the sword in time of war. 21You will be safe from slander and have no fear when destruction comes. 22You will laugh at destruction and famine; wild animals will not terrify

you. 23You will be at peace with the stones of the field, and its wild animals will be at peace with you. 24You will know that your home is safe." Job 5:17-24

"We have studied life and found all this to be true. Listen to my counsel, and apply it to yourself." Job 5:27

I beautified my sins by being corrected by God. I beautified my sins by being at peace with what and who hurt me. I acknowledged my weaknesses, embraced my flaws, spiritually cleansed energy, repented, honored my parents, and took full accountability. I beautified my sins by building a closer relationship with God to strengthen my faith and truly understand the definition of forgiveness and love. Without my spiritual growth, I don't know where I would be today. What I do know is that I would still be lost, confused, and in the same repetitive cycle looking for an escape. I had tried everything, literally everything, and nothing worked for me. I tried sex, drugs, alcohol, partying, partnership, lowering self, mentors, therapy, and church, but nothing was equivalent to knowing, understanding, and hearing from God for myself. Understanding relationship is more important than religion. I listened to endless preachers preach sermons Sunday after Sunday and listened to several people give me advice, but it still never filled my empty cup. I needed to be spiritually fed and challenged but that was what I was missing most. Surrounding myself in a circle that only fit my broken piece and not my masterpiece. I beautified my sins by learning to stop pointing the finger at others and look at myself and my broken pieces. A lot of my pain was self-inflicted. That is something we don't like to admit. Again, I'm talking about accountability. Many of my life choices were bluntly wrong. If only I had a more mature mentality, but that's the beauty in growth!

"When I was a child, I talked like a child, I thought like a child, I reasoned like a child; when I became a man, I did away childish things. 12For now (in this time of imperfection) we see in a mirror dimly (a blurred reflection, a riddle, an enigma), but then (when the time of perfection comes we will see reality) face to face. Now I know in part (just in fragments), but then I will know fully, just as I have been fully known (by God).13 And now there remain: faith (abiding trust in God and His promises), hope (confident expectation of eternal salvation), love (unselfish love for others growing out of God's love for me), these three (the choicest graces); but the greatest of these is love." 1 Corinthians 13:11-13

Reflect on this passage. Now, I challenge you to think about what you still hold on to that transpired in your life as a child. What keeps you in bondage, causing you to act in a childish manner? Know that when I refer to a child, I do not just mean a minor. When you look in the mirror, what causes your broken pieces? Once you've dug down to your roots to figure out where it all began, were you just a child (minor) or an adult responding as a child?

_____
_____
_____
_____

_____
_____
_____
_____
_____
_____

One day, I was on Instagram and came across a post that said, "Ultra independence is a coping mechanism we develop when we've learned it's not safe to trust love or when we are terrified to lose ourselves in another. We aren't meant to do it alone. We are wounded in relationships, and we heal in relationships." How ironic that I came across this scripture and post in the same week.

When I reflect on 1 Corinthians 13:11, I'm reminded of how I became a woman in Christ and had to put away the childish things of the world in my mind. I had to stop the immature acts and become a woman who took responsibility for healing from my broken pieces that were still captive inside my mind. I still saw shattered pieces in the mirror every day. Failing to see the perfect shattered-free me, the way God viewed Key, was my incentive to keep working. God's plan for me wasn't my reality until I put away my childish things. It was then that I was able to learn and grow into the real definition of love.

We are wounded in relationships. Any relationship can wound us, whether it be an intimate, friendship, association, church, work, or even family relationship. We can be hurt while connected in any form or manner. Putting our faith and trust in someone who fails us tends to make us become guarded. After the broken trust, we don't want to let someone else in, we become afraid to trust, or love again. As a result, we become a strong, independent person. That's just a way to ignore, cope with, and hide our inner hurt, which creates more shattered pieces in the mirror. We either ignore the trauma by running into the arms of another, or we seclude ourselves. When we are afraid of getting hurt again, we hide our hearts.

I know you may be wondering, Well, Kiawana, what are you saying? What I am saying is to heal from your shattered and broken pieces. Know your worth, and see yourself the way God sees you. Honestly, you'll never get to that place of peace until you get right with Him. This is where you heal in relationship with God.

I had all the faith and hope in the world that everything would be made anew. I would be at peace. I would be free. My love life would improve, and everything would get better. While I had faith and hope, I still had shattered pieces because I carried bitterness and hatred instead of forgiveness and love. I didn't have a committed relationship with God and that was one that I needed the most.

I.D.E.N.T.I.T.Y.

"Therefore, if anyone is in Christ (that is, grafted in, joined to Him by faith in Him as Savior), he is a new creature (reborn and renewed by the Holy Spirit); the old things (the previous moral and spiritual condition) have passed away. Behold, new things have come (because spiritual awakening brings a new life). But all these things are from God, who reconciled us to Himself through Christ (making us acceptable to Him) and gave us the ministry of reconciliation (so that by our example we might bring others to Him). 2 Corinthians 5:17-18

I'm not liable to sin
I'm flawless, sinless, and virtuous
I'm ready to make this a trend
Perfect in all His ways, pure, exemplary for the Kingdom

A woman of Impeccable character, I am the I of my Identity!

Punished for my actions as any Father that loves His child would do

I'm dedicated, daring, and zealous

My sinful wills have been rebuked and I have been trained to educate, too

I am brilliant, extraordinary

One of God's minority

I have been Disciplined; I am the D of my iDentity!

Styled in His grace and mercy

With elegance and class

Representing God's royalty

Some think I'm eccentric

Which is comedy to me

My theology is Christocentric

And I am an Effervescent woman; I am the E of my idEntity!

Nurturing, nourished, caregiver

I learned how to love with my heart rather than with my mind

I appreciate the beauty of not receiving; I'm the striver

Grateful for the way how I'm designed

I am Noteworthy; I am the N of my ideNtity!

I remember being so tense, feared the thought of being touched

So broken and brittle

No longer using the world being crutched

A smile so bright because I know what is written
I am a Tranquil woman; I am the T of my idenTity!
Ironical, I am a reflection of my Father
Perfectly flawed, but I'm destined to make it right
Not going down without a fight
I know that it all will get better
I am Impervious to the naysayers; I am the I of my identIty!
Transparent, feisty, determined, and goal-oriented
A fragrance of my Father, I'm so scented
But I'm resented because I'm not who I used to be
But I can't help it; I would rather be the true and free Key
I am a Trendy Tenacious woman; I am the T of my identiTy!
Being resented, I sometimes yonder
But remember that my purpose is bigger than me
The negativity, why even bother?
The favor of the Lord rest upon me
I am a Yielding woman; I am the Y of my identitY!

As bad as I would like to put the pen down to end this book, Beautifying Sins, I have the urge to give you more. No one can beautify anything about self if one does not know what or who they are. So, I ask you, do you know your IDENTITY? Do you know what and who you are? What do you think about yourself and the characteristics that define you?

Who are you?

_____
_____
_____
_____
_____

The reason I asked who you are is to allow you to be transparent with yourself. Did you write who you desire to be, continuing to hide behind this false identity? Or did you identify and write who you are? I have realized from personal experience and observations that embracing a false identity has become society's biggest weakness. Why? Because it robs us from our lives to make dreams a reality. It's important to have a connection with something greater than you.

This is where your spiritual identity comes in. Spiritual IDENTITY (awakening), for lack of a better word, is to rid yourself of ego and connect with a higher spirit to rise to a higher level within. I know you are saying, But why? I am not even spiritual. Having a personal sense of spirituality is one of the most important steps to happiness. Spiritual identity meaning can go deep into a sense that gives life. Without it, life can seem empty and without purpose. It occurs when, for whatever reason, your ego finally let's go and allows the spirit to move within you.

Let me ask you a question. Do you know what your life's purpose is? If you said no or thought of an obnoxious reason, that's ok. However, I encourage you to get connected to your spiritual identity.

There are many levels of identity, my God! The beginning stage (ego), the process, the current, and the final. Where are you? Are you ready to glow, grow, and evolve?

Dear Father God,

You are an amazing, omnipotent, gracious, most powerful, and righteous God. You are perfect in all of Your ways. You make no mistakes nor lead any of us the wrong way. And for that, Father God, I say thank You. I thank You in advance for the way You will show Your face upon Your children. Many souls will cry out to You for deliverance and repentance. I thank you for not letting any of us go when we deserved to be released. I thank You for still loving us even when we were hurt by love. I thank You for not judging us and looking beyond our faults and flaws even when we deserve to be condemned.

Now, God, I stand in the gap for my fellow brothers and sisters. Help them to look in the mirror and see themselves the way You see them. Let them know that you are doing a new thing in their lives and here on Earth. Mend every shattered piece to see perfection as You see in us. Allow them to pay attention and not miss your presence, oh Father God.

I pray now, God, as a sign of surrendering. Forgive us, oh God, for our sinful ways. Forgive us, oh God, for our lustful thoughts. Oh God, forgive us for our brokenness and bitterness. Forgive us, God, for coping through turbulence instead of changing in the midst of it. Forgive us for putting the world before You instead of putting the world behind You. Forgive us for holding onto grudges, past pain, hurt, and abuse.

Now, God, I lift every family member in prayer. Oh God, break generational chains. God, break generational curses. Father, break the cycle and allow them to end with me. I don't want to be like them, oh God. I desire to be different; my heart thirsts to be different; I hunger to be different.

Do Your works through me, oh God, and send me to Your land that the world will humble themselves and pray and seek Your face, oh God. I pray that the world sees me and believes in You. Oh God, I pray that they see how You made right my wrongs for your glory, Father God. Let Your children understand that there is a purpose in our pain, Father God, and there is a reason for every season. Fix my mirror that the world would see You through me. Fix our lenses that our hearts would rely on You. Fix my mirror to know and understand my true identity, as You have called me to be. Father God, guide us to acknowledge our weakness. Help us to embrace our weakness and wash us clean from all of our childish things. Help us to walk in pure maturity to see Your face, oh God.

Now, Lord Jesus, I take a moment to admit that I am a sinner, and, Father, I ask for Your forgiveness. I believe You died on the cross for my sins and rose from the dead. Today, I turn away from childish, sinful things, and I invite You to take over my heart and my life. Purify me, oh God. Cleanse me, oh God. Have Your will and Your way. I want to trust and follow You as my Lord and Savior. I am guilty of my sins, but because I have been cleansed and I am committed and dedicated to You, that's what makes me beautiful. Not only am I guilty and have been cleansed, but I am dedicated and committed to change, grow, and evolve. I am committed to grow, glow, evolve into who You say that I am. Thank You for Your grace and mercy and for showing Your face to me. I'm not perfect, and I make mistakes, but that's why I need your strength, Father God, to carry me through. In my immature moments, God, give me the wisdom and discernment that I need from You. I declare and decree from this day forward our broken pieces are Your masterpiece. It is so, the only reason I'm here today is because you love me, I honor You, I am thankful, I am grateful, and I will glorify Your name forever! Even when my days get hard and life seems not to make sense, I know that You have a plan and purpose destined for me. So I'm committed to growing, glowing, and evolving in You.

Love always,
A little sinner like me!

Acknowledgements

I would be wrong if I didn't start my acknowledgments off by first giving honor to God, who is the head of my life. In all honesty, I am grateful. I owe God everything, and I thank Him for choosing me. It's seldom for youth to have a business where they are completely vulnerable and exalt the name of Jesus in the midst of everything. I will forever boast about the favor that He has shown me repeatedly, and I am beyond honored.

To my loving, adorable, and bubbly daughter, Azariah Malia, Mommy loves you. I know my sacrifices may not make sense to you now, but I promise in 2020 you will understand. To my family, friends, and supporters, words cannot measure my gratitude towards you. Thank you for praying for me, believing in me, and for supporting me. I love you!

At the end of 2017, while wavering in my faith, I stumbled upon The House of Healing DMV. I told myself and God that once He took my childhood best friend away from me, I would never be involved in church or get attached to another pastor again. I used toxic traits to cope with my grief. I believed God had failed me and was beyond cruel to take the life of someone who I felt was least deserving to go. When I tell you being under the leadership of Pastor Joseph and LaQuisha Brown has been life-changing, I cannot begin to explain and go in-depth to describe it. I literally felt myself dying on the inside from being so lost. To find loving, genuine, welcoming, challenging, and transparent pastors has been the best encounter to experience during my brokenness. I am honored, grateful, and thankful that God has placed me in my church home and blessed me with the divine connection between my pastors and me. Poppa J, I thank you so much for welcoming me with open arms and being willing to do the foreword for Beautifying Sins! I love you immensely.

To my Inspirers, thank you so much for your continuous love and support. You mean the world to me. I love you and I am grateful for you!

About The Author

Life can be brutal, unforgiving, and beautiful all at the same time. For Kiawana "Key" Leaf, she's experienced this and a whole lot more. A self-made entrepreneur, author, actress, and inspirational speaker, Kiawana aspires to inspire, empower, and embrace millennials across the nation. To heal from traumatic events in their life, find, and fulfill their purpose and women who are survivors of domestic abuse through her first business venture, Empower Too Inspire, LLC. The foundation of Empower Too Inspire is built on Women's Empowerment and Kingdom Advancement.

Kiawana is a rising star who was featured on TV One's "For My Man" and Ari Squires' soul stirring documentary "No More Chains 2". While life has thrown many obstacles her way, Kiawana's faith in God has never wavered. She dedicated her life to Jesus Christ at the age of twelve. Kiawana's greatest inspiration comes from her greatest joy–her daughter, Azariah. Kiawana looks forward to being an inspiration to many who are seeking healing and spiritual growth. It is her dream, vision, purpose, and power to Empower Too Inspire!

Contact Info:
Business Website: www.empowertooinspire.org

Author Website: www.kiawanaleaf.com

Business/Author Email:
Kiawanaleaf@empowertooinspire.org

Facebook: Kiawana Leaf

Instagram: @Kiawana___ & @Empowertooinspire

www.ingramcontent.com/pod-product-compliance
Lightning Source LLC
Chambersburg PA
CBHW061222070526
44584CB00029B/3950